EVOLVING TECHNOLOGY

# THE EVOLUTION OF AGRICULTURAL TECHNOLOGY



PAULA MARIE

Britannica Educational Publishing
IN ASSOCIATION WITH
ROSEN
EDUCATIONAL SERVICES

Published in 2019 by Britannica Educational Publishing (a trademark of Encyclopædia Britannica, Inc.) in association with The Rosen Publishing Group, Inc.
29 East 21st Street, New York, NY 10010



Distributed exclusively by Rosen Publishing.
To see additional Britannica Educational Publishing titles, go to rosenpublishing.com.

First Edition

**Britannica Educational Publishing**
J.E. Luebering: Executive Director, Core Editorial
Andrea R. Field: Managing Editor, Compton's by Britannica

**Rosen Publishing**
Bernadette Davis: Editor
Nelson Sá: Art Director
Brian Garvey: Series Designer/Book Layout
Cindy Reiman: Photography Manager
Ellina Litmanovich: Photo Researcher

**Library of Congress Cataloging-in-Publication Data**

Names: Marie, Paula, author.
Title: The evolution of agricultural technology / Paula Marie.
Description: New York : Britannica Educational Publishing, in Association with Rosen Educational Services, 2019. | Series: Evolving technology | Includes bibliographical references and index. | Audience: Grades 5-8.
Identifiers: LCCN 2017044408| ISBN 9781538302798 (library bound : alk. paper) | ISBN 9781538302804 (pbk. : alk. paper)
Subjects: LCSH: Agriculture—History—Juvenile literature. | Agricultural innovations—History—Juvenile literature.
Classification: LCC S419 .J637 2018 | DDC 338.1—dc23
LC record available at https://lccn.loc.gov/2017044408

*Manufactured in the United States of America*

**Photo credits**: Cover (left to right) vectorx2263/Shutterstock.com, Somchai Sanvongchaiya/Shutterstock.com, Perception7/Shutterstock.com; cover, back cover, pp. 4-5 (background), 7, 21, 29, 36, 46 spainter_vfx/Shutterstock.com; p. 5 © Dr. Nigel Smith/The Hutchison Library; p. 11 PHB.cz/Fotolia; p. 13 © R.C. Hunt/Encyclopædia Britannica, Inc.; p. 15 Eye Ubiquitous/Universal Images Group/Getty Images; pp. 19, 48 Encyclopædia Britannica, Inc.; p. 22 Juan Mabromata/AFP/Getty Images; p. 24 Edward S. Curtis Collection/Library of Congress, Washington, D.C. (cph 3a16196); p. 25 wanida tubtawee/Shutterstock.com; p. 28 © Photos.com/Jupiterimages; p. 31 small1/Shutterstock.com; p. 33 © USDA Agricultural Research Station; p. 34 AdstockRF; p. 40 Mark Agnor/Shutterstock.com; p. 41 NIAID; p. 43 Robert Pernell/Shutterstock.com; pp. 44–45 ChiccoDodiFC/Fotolia; p. 50 Andia/Universal Images Group/Getty Images; p. 53 NurPhoto/Getty Images; p. 55 Alberto Pizzoli/AFP/Getty Images.

# CONTENTS

# INTRODUCTION

People have always used technology to help themselves get food and eat it—that is, if we consider that technology includes everything from basic stone tools to advanced computer programs. Today, people have access to an amazing variety of foods from all over the world, partly thanks to modern technology and partly because of ancient inventions. However, agricultural technology has still not solved problems like famine and malnutrition, and many people have unequal access to nutritious foods. These and additional challenges, such as global warming, mean that sustainable agriculture will be vital to our future.

Agriculture has no single, simple origin. It developed gradually and independently in many regions of the world. People everywhere were already adept at finding wild plants and animals they could eat. As they turned from gathering wild foods, as well as hunting and fishing, to agriculture, they developed new kinds of tools and ways of creating food. In addition to stone tools, they made tools out of antlers and bones, posts and digging sticks out of wood, fishing nets out of plant fibers, storage containers out of gourds, and baskets out of grass and leaves. Over many thousands of years people made more efficient tools, and they became more organized at growing food.

People domesticated a wide variety of plants and animals at different times. Parts of the Middle East have traces of grain farming from thousands of years ago. Agriculture might have begun even earlier in Southeast Asia. Both of those areas were rich in animals suitable for domestication and in varieties of plants, and both had mild climates. Additionally, agriculture was developed in East Asia and in the Americas thousands of years ago.

These African farms in Burundi grow coffee for export as well as crops to support many more people than could be fed by hunting and gathering.

People didn't always domesticate the animals around them, especially those in water. Sometimes trapping animals or raising them in enclosures was easier than completely domesticating them. People built fish weirs to trap fish in rivers and estuaries. They modified beaches to increase the size of the habitat for marine life like clams and crabs.

When people began to domesticate animals, they chose species that were already somewhat calm around humans. Then, over time, they selectively bred them to favor different traits that made the animals more docile, or easier to control. Humans chose to raise and eat mostly herbivores (plant eaters). They observed over countless generations that carnivores (meat eaters) were difficult to capture and control.

Surrounded by fields where plants and animals were raised, family homes grew over time into villages or towns and eventually cities. Ultimately, farming and related technologies helped lead to the development of modern civilization.

## Chapter 1

# STONE AGE ORIGINS OF AGRICULTURE

From the earliest times, agriculture has included raising both crops and animals. Before agriculture became well established, hunter-gatherers and fishers had to seek out plants and animals useful to them. Wild fruits, nuts, and berries were probably the first plant foods of ancient peoples. Later, humans learned to dig up roots and scrape or pound them to a paste for eating. Then, as people ate some plants more than others, they threw the unusable remains onto the ground nearby. As a result, the seeds of these preferred species became more likely to sprout close to human settlements.

The pattern continued as some varieties of fruits, vegetables, and grains began to be used more often than others. In a similar way, some animals began to risk coming closer to human villages, and humans showed more tolerance for certain of these animal "neighbors" than others. This means that slowly, but in not-quite random ways, natural selection gave humans a boost in the direction of agriculture.

As natural selection made some plants and animals more compatible with human life, and vice versa, people learned to favor some species to a greater degree. In other words, people helped certain plants and animals reproduce in a process we now call artificial selection—a key to domestication. People learned to select those varieties of wild plant species that had desirable features—such as large kernels or fruits. They also began to influence the diets and behaviors of the animals around them.

Tools have always been key to agricultural progress. People began using stone tools millions of years ago in Africa. Eventually this technology—including stone digging tools, meat scrapers, axes, and spear points—spread around the world. People also gathered and prepared food with tools of bone, antler, ivory, and perishable materials such as wood that we have seldom found in excavations. Archaeologists have found 160,000-year-old grindstones that held traces of starch because they were used to grind seeds. Fishing hooks and spears are evidence from forty thousand years ago that people were skilled at finding food in rivers and lakes and ocean shorelines.

## THE FIRST DOMESTICATED ANIMALS AND PLANTS

Over many thousands of years, people favored certain plants and animals over others. Eventually they learned to grow plants for food, medicine, clothing, and shelter in areas set aside for that purpose. Because it made life much easier for many people, it became the preferred way of fulfilling a basic human need. People also discovered that there were particular advantages to caring for animals in flocks and herds. These changes marked the gradual beginning of agriculture.

The first domesticated animals were dogs. Wolves that scavenged near human communities were their ancestors. In a sense, the wolves began to domesticate themselves before humans even planned to do so, because wolves that could peacefully live near humans began to eat more regularly. (Meanwhile, many could not—so other wolves continued on as a separate, wild species.) Those wolves that were more compatible with humans gradually became domesticated between thirty and fifteen thousand years ago in East Asia and the Middle East. In archaeological excavations, their bones show that they underwent changes as they became tamer—and as their diets changed as well. Over the millennia since then, humans have bred dogs into different groups called breeds, with an amazing variety of sizes, skull shapes, colors, and ways of behaving. As a result of their close connections with humans, dogs are far better at understanding human intentions, such as our gestures (pointing) and our emotional reactions, than wolves; dogs are even better at this than our closest primate relatives, chimpanzees and gorillas. The old saying, "Dog is Man's best friend" or (in updated language) "Dogs are humans' best friends," is backed up by millennia of evidence.

Grazing animals such as goats, gazelles, and sheep were domesticated before plants were farmed in the Middle East. Chickens were domesticated in Southeast Asia at about the same time as the grazing animals of the Middle East. Wild tarpans were domesticated into the horses we know today, and wild oxen (aurochs) became today's cattle. Rather than keeping herds of all of these animals in one place,

Sheep and goats were among the first animals to be domesticated because these herd animals live together in flocks and because they eat grass and scrubby bushes.

many societies became pastoral, herding flocks long distances to find fresh grass fields. Larger domesticated animals were used for food and hides and as draft animals, pulling carts and eventually plows.

Early farmers set pieces of a plant—roots, buds, leaves, underground stems—in the ground to produce more plants like the parent. This is a process we now call vegetative reproduction. They eventually learned to replant other types each year, usu-

## THE PLOW AND THE SICKLE

Tools for growing and harvesting grain are older than we once thought. The first plows were either basic stone tools or sharpened sticks, but archaeologists rarely find preserved wood. Digging sticks were used to poke holes in the soil or dragged to make a furrow when planting seeds. Plowing small fields with a digging stick was tiring work. Planters could harvest grain with a sharp flint knife in one hand to cut through the stems, but a sickle is more efficient. Early sickles for harvesting grain were jawbones of an ungulate such as deer, from the Neolithic ("new" Stone Age) era some fourteen thousand years ago.

ally from seeds. Today we call these kinds of plants "annuals." Early farmers learned to save seeds from their best plants to sow for the next year's crop. By patient selection from one season to the next, the farmers gradually improved the species. This is how wild grasses became the ancestors of modern grains, beginning about 10,500 years ago in the Middle East.

In East Asia, genetic and archaeological evidence suggest that the earliest rice was domes-

People domesticated different kinds of grains to grow in various climate zones, such as rice for these flooded fields in China.

ticated in the Yangtze River region in China about nine thousand to eight thousand years ago. Rice is planted in flooded fields that are allowed to dry up gradually as the plants grow.

Early crops in the Middle East were emmer wheat and einkorn wheat. They were first grown at least twelve thousand years ago.

In Africa the first large-scale crops were the grains teff, millet, and sorghum. Later, a variety of beans was grown as well. In Australia, wild millet was the grain that was farmed. People in the Americas grew rice, teosinte (an ancestor of maize), and in South America, quinoa and brome grass.

## MANAGING ANIMAL AND PLANT RESOURCES IN THE AMERICAS

In many parts of the Americas between thirty thousand and fourteen thousand years ago, people established villages at coastal and inland sites. Stone tools, carved bones and antlers, plant seeds, and the bones of domesticated dogs of several breeds have been found at these village sites.

People living along seashores often gathered seaweed and invertebrates at low tide. They learned how to improve the habitat for intertidal life and how to provide themselves with reliable seafood. The streams where salmon spawned were maintained and altered to improve access to these fish. Along the coast, some villages harvested sea mammals like otters, seals, and even whales with spears and ropes.

These mammals were a resource that people hunted sustainably for thousands of years. The human populations of the time were too limited to slaughter large numbers of prey at once—unlike

In Peru, these farmers are planting corn in their field by hand, using a traditional wooden plow pulled by oxen.

our fishing and hunting technologies today, which have pushed some of these species to the brink of extinction.

Fishing technology dates to at least seven thousand years ago in some Pacific Northwest coastal locations. Wooden tools are rarely preserved, but archaeologists have found fishhooks and spearheads of bone, as well as stone net weights. There is also evidence of construction of stone and wooden weirs and traps in many places in the Americas.

People practiced farming with gardens and small fields where the climate and resources were favorable. In what is now southern Mexico, about ten thousand years ago, maize (corn) was first cultivated. It was harvested and dried for winter use and kept in underground storage granaries lined with dried grasses. Over the next thousands of years, this domesticated maize began to spread to other areas, becoming an important part of the religions and diets of Central, North, and South American peoples.

In what is now Illinois, seven thousand years ago, native peoples were farming squash. Other crops in the American Midwest included sunflowers, goosefoot, and marsh elder. At about the same time, llamas and alpacas were being domesticated in South America. However, these animals could not carry much weight or pull plows—so they were not useful as draft animals in the ways that oxen, cattle, and horses were in Eurasia.

About five thousand years ago, maize was brought into what is now the United States, and it was brought southward to the Andes Mountains of South America as well. Farming techniques for many other crops spread north from Mexico into the southwestern United States around four thousand years ago.

By that time in many parts of the Americas, people were tilling gardens to plant root vegetables such as camas bulbs on Canada's west coast or potatoes in the highlands of Bolivia and Peru.

## FARMING IN THE MEDITERRANEAN AND MIDDLE EAST

As the food supply became more consistent, each person's farmwork raised enough food to feed more than one person. Some people were free to do other things besides farming and hunting. Many of them chose to live in towns and cities, using their talents in various ways, including becoming experts in different trades. They made a variety of goods, which they could trade with the farmers for food. This practice began the division of labor into the rural farming community and the urban industrial complex, a fundamental partnership that still exists worldwide. Early agriculture also began changing the world's climate, as browsing goats and sheep ate enough greenery to change vegetation and evaporation patterns.

Mesopotamia was called the cradle of civilization because of its early farms and cities. Ancient Mesopotamian cultures, including those of Sumeria, Babylonia, Assyria, and Chaldea, developed an increasingly complex and rich agricultural system. These people of the Fertile Crescent region made use of irrigation technology such as canals and ditches that carried water from reservoirs into fields.

The people managed the planting and harvesting of grains so efficiently that they helped lead to the development of the world's first cities. A related factor was the brewing of beer, which went hand-in-hand with farming technology—perhaps even leading the way. Long before microscopic germs were understood (long before they were first seen in microscopes), beer was produced by boiling and fermenting water and grains, making a liquid that was free of germs. In contrast, water supplies in towns and cities were unsafe because of pollution from human and animal waste.

Cats seem to have become domesticated in the Middle East around the same time that humans farmed and stored a variety of grains. Mice and rats made the most of this food opportunity, and several varieties of wild cats preyed on those rodents. House cats are descended from the smallest species of these wild cats. Their bones, excavated from these early sites, show changes as they became domesticated.

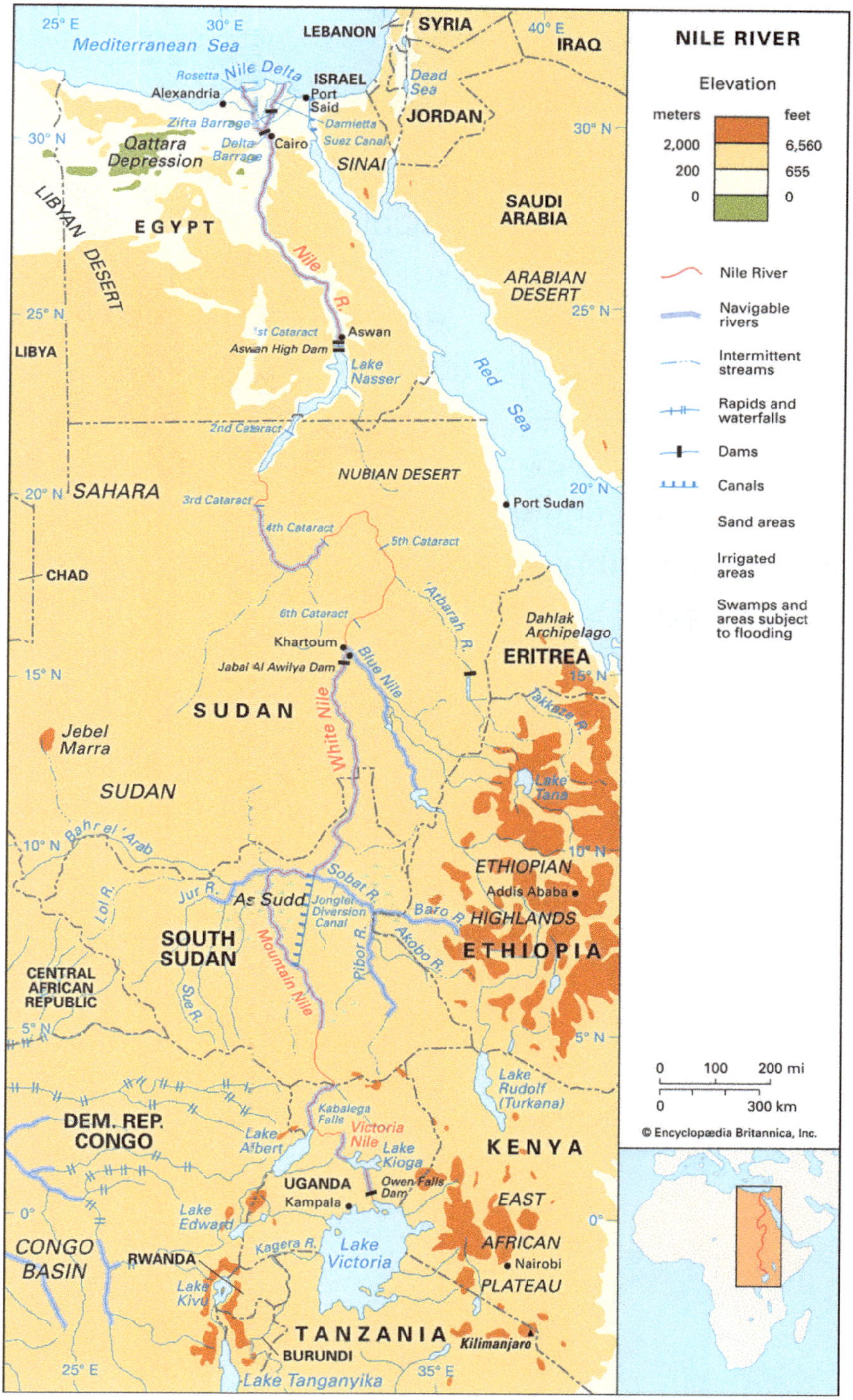


Long before twentieth-century construction of the Aswan Dam, the ancient Egyptian civilization grew along the Nile River, where annual floods watered and fertilized fields.

Early crops in the Middle East included grains such as wheat, oats, rye, barley, and millet. Later legumes such as peas, lentils, chickpeas, and beans developed there. In addition, people deliberately planted vegetable crops, including kale, cabbage, and turnips. Grapes, olives, dates, apples, pears, cherries, and figs were among early domesticated fruits. Early crops in East Asia included millet, rice, cabbage, and soybeans.

By the time Egypt was ruled by the pharaohs four thousand years ago, farmers in the Nile River valley had fine agricultural technology for raising crops and livestock, including an efficient grain distribution program. Among the records from the building of the great pyramids were invoices for rations of grain, onions, olive oil, and beer for workers.

## Chapter 2

# TRADITIONAL AGRICULTURE OF NATIVE PEOPLES OF THE AMERICAS

Native peoples of North and South America (also variously called American Indians, Native Americans, or First Nations) have used agricultural technology when managing their resources for thousands of years, at least since the end of the last Ice Age. Traditional methods for raising and harvesting food varied in different regions. Digging sticks were used in most places. They managed plants and animals, both domesticated and wild; however, no animals pulled plows because large domesticated animals were not available. Harvest sickles and knives were made of flint or bone. Native peoples maintained meadows and prairies and managed forests and watersheds extending far into wilderness areas that were less frequently traveled.

## MANAGING THE LAND

People learned to manage forests for several purposes. In many places fire was used instead of axes and saws to clear brush and trees. In South America the ancestors of the Guaraní and other native peoples cleared bands of forests for croplands along the Amazon and other rivers. The soil along the Amazon is usually not fertile because heavy rains wash much of the minerals away, so people improved the earth

In the Americas, native peoples used controlled burning, which fertilized the soil and maintained cropland by clearing away brush and trees.

in their garden plots and fields. By seven thousand years ago, they had learned to build up the soil with compost, ashes, and biochar, a charcoal made by burning wood and agricultural waste. These added organic nutrients, producing what is now called *terra preta do Indio*: a rich black soil that remains fertile in sites throughout the rainforest.

On the Pacific Northwest Coast, people modified red cedar and other trees by pulling bark strips for making clothing. They also dug spruce roots for making baskets. People learned to split lumber, sometimes from living cedar trees, to construct homes from planks of wood. Boats were carved up to a hundred feet long, beginning with a standing tree.

## CAPTURING AND STORING FISH

Fishing was done with specialized tools. There were lines and hooks of bone or wood for various kinds of fish, from small to large. Nets, fish traps, and weirs were made of spruce and cedar roots, with floats and stone weights, in various sizes up to large enough to span a river. Spears were also used in river canyons to catch salmon swimming upstream.

In the Aleutian Islands, Aleut or Unangan people traditionally built light boats called *iqyax* or baidarkas (kayaks) to use when fishing or hunting sea mammals.

When herring spawned in ocean shallows, people collected the eggs. They either ate them fresh or dried them on branches and seaweed for storage. Herring themselves were caught on a rake-like pole with several sharp points and shaken off into a canoe. Little eulachon or candlefish were caught in nets and rendered for their strongly flavored, vitamin-rich oil, which was traded inland for 1,000 miles (1,600 kilometers) or more.

Technology for storing fish was specialized, too. On wooden racks, fish were dried in the wind or smoked above a fire. Smoked fish was stored in boxes made of bent wood and in tightly woven baskets.

Clam gardens were built on some seashores from Alaska to Washington state. These were not "gardens" in a traditional sense. Instead, they were beach terraces extended to improve habitat for clams. Some clam gardens were built three thousand years ago, but some may be much older. They are called "wuxwuthin" by the Tla'amin people, whose ancestors smoked clams and strung them on cords, to trade them with groups inland.

First Nation people on North America's Pacific Coast construct walls along beaches to increase habitat for raising clams and other seafood.

## ANIMALS AND THEIR WOOL

Native peoples of the Americas traditionally managed land animals in many ways. They had dogs throughout the Americas in breeds as diverse as huskies, Chihuahuas, and Salish wool dogs. They succeeded in managing and sustaining wild populations of other animals for reliable harvests instead of keeping livestock on farms. In the Pacific Northwest, blankets were made from mountain goat wool shed in spring and collected from hillsides above villages.

The Salish people on the coasts added fur from wool dogs (Salish dogs). They kept these dogs isolated from other dogs to preserve a recessive genetic trait for wooly fur. They fed them meat scraps with added elk fat and fish oil. Oral histories suggest that these traditions date back thousands of years, perhaps to the last Ice Age.

In South America, domesticated animals seven thousand years ago included llamas and alpacas for beasts of burden, although they were not strong enough to carry people or pull plows. They were also eaten and kept for their wool. Guinea pigs were raised for food, often by keeping them in small trenches or clay pits within family homes.

## FOOD TOOLS

Native peoples of the Americas had a particular set of tools that they relied on. They made tools for digging by attaching wood poles to sharpened stone, bone, or ivory points. Stone could also be shaped into knives and cutting edges. Some could be ground into bowls and mortar and pestle.

## THE THREE SISTERS

Among native peoples of the Americas a traditional method of companion planting—the "three sisters" of maize (corn) with beans and squash—has been used for at least one thousand years. Rather than planting separate rows, farmers prepare small mounds of tilled earth. Two or three maize seeds, bean seeds, and squash seeds are planted in each mound. The cornstalk grows straight and tall, providing a support for the bean vine to climb. The bean plant helps the maize as well. We now know that it pulls nitrogen from the air and fixes it into nodules on its roots, fertilizing the soil for the maize. The big squash leaves shade the ground as a natural cover. This cover reduces weed growth, keeps the mound cool during hot weather, and saves water by reducing evaporation from the mound. These "three sisters" have provided a balanced diet with a surplus of protein and vitamins.

For harvesting food, many varieties of basket were made from local materials: spruce roots, grasses, pine needles, and more. Baskets and mats

Baskets were not only practical but could have traditionally meaningful designs, like this harvesting basket made by Wappo people from Napa Valley, California.

could be open weave like a strainer or tightly woven and even lined with clay to make them watertight. Some people kept preserved food in lasting containers made of wood or pottery or hollowed out granaries in stone. Oil could be kept in skins and pottery jugs. Stored food was eaten during late winter, traded, or given as gifts during ceremonies.

Chapter 3

# UNDER THE PLOW AND FENCE

During the Greek and Roman eras in the Mediterranean region, about three to two thousand years ago, sophisticated farming tools were made for tilling, cultivating, and harvesting field crops. The Greeks also established botany as a science in that era. However, social upheavals in the Roman Empire kept agricultural technology inferior to that of the Egyptians and East Asians.

## CREATING A METHODOLOGY OF FARMING

About 200 BCE, the Roman author Cato wrote *De agricultura* on practical aspects of crop and livestock management. This helped lead to larger farms, with slaves for workers and managers. The surplus food was moved swiftly along Roman roads to its large cities and army camps.

After about 100 BCE, Roman arborists learned grafting and budding to manage tree fruits. They utilized crop rotation and fertilizer (manure) regularly. The Romans also built an early type of greenhouse. Their massive aqueduct system, meanwhile, brought freshwater from miles away to Rome.

The Middle East and East Asia were centers of technological advance before and after the classical Greek and Roman periods. They managed enormous crops of rice and other grains, as well as herds of horses and sheep. Asia's agricultural surpluses gave it the largest cities in the world for many centuries.

## SELECTIVE BREEDING

Selective breeding has been done since agriculture began. It occurs when people choose which plants or animals may breed and which they will make sterile. By selective breeding, people have chosen qualities that they need, such as wheat having bigger seeds than wild grasses. Sheep were selectively bred for either their meat or their wool.

Cattle were selectively bred for either meat production or milk production. Farming communities would keep only a few bulls, boars, rams, or stal-

Most young male farm animals are gelded after careful selection of only a few males that will be allowed to breed.

lions. They would allow only the healthiest or largest male animals to breed with the entire herd of cows. Meanwhile, they only kept females whose offspring were calm and healthy.

Record keeping was particularly important for horses, as they were being bred for various purposes, from small ponies to huge Shire draft horses as well as warhorses and racehorses. In England, breeding records date back before the Domesday Book and William the Conqueror's reign in 1066 CE.

## EARLY CIVIL ENGINEERING

Two thousand years ago, in both Asia and Europe, engineers built extensive canal and irrigation systems. A thousand years ago similar systems were built in Mexico and in the US Southwest. Complex systems of terraced fields were eventually built up in places as distant as the mountains of China, India, and South America. Farmers around the world since then have continued to shape their land to manage water resources, increase production, and reduce erosion.

Inland in Mexico and in South America, extensive patterns of "raised fields" were constructed, mostly by human labor (without beasts of burden). They were built to irrigate and keep crops warm during cold, frosty nights. Sometimes even the ocean has been tamed, as civil engineering has contributed to agricultural technology, as with the vast polder system in the Netherlands.

## AGRICULTURAL REVOLUTION

By the end of the Middle Ages in the 1500s CE, most of the tillable land of Europe was cleared, drained,

Grapes have been selectively bred and traditionally grown in Europe since before the time of ancient Greece and the Roman Empire.

and in cultivation. Meanwhile, crops such as tomatoes and potatoes were brought to Europe from the Americas for the first time. New industries arose, creating markets for such crops as sugarcane, hemp, flax, vegetable oils, and dyes. Violence also accompanied some shifts as, for example, when noble landowners in England forced peasants off the "commons," shared pastures where they had traditionally kept animals. Instead of commons, these communities now had "enclosures" or enclosed fields, controlled by the wealthy nobles. These transitions from medieval to modern agricultural practices, including the less honest and abusive changes, were later called the Agricultural Revolution.

With this revolution, each plant and plot of land was increasingly managed. Short-stalked varieties

## DISRUPTION AND PROGRESS

Because of colonialism during the 1700s and 1800s, European settlers exterminated nearly all the wandering herds of bison in North America and some other ungulates in other parts of the world. With traditional animal management systems disrupted, colonial governments helped European immigrants develop farms and plantations. Their large herds of cattle could eat rangeland bare of grasses and brush. Later, sheep farmers in some areas added to the disruption, as they fenced off areas formerly open to cattle ranchers.

North American bison are stronger, bigger, and more independent than cattle selectively bred for beef or dairy production.

of wheat were for animal food and bales of straw, used to line stables and to mulch garden plots. Long-stalked varieties growing up to nine feet tall were used for thatching roofs. Durum wheat had hard kernels for grinding into flour to make pasta and bread.

New farming systems of enclosed fields, crop rotation, and keeping animals in stalls became more efficient with time. Plows were improved, and eventually mechanical seed sowers, threshers, and harvesters were introduced.

Scientific plant breeding did not begin until the discovery of the principles of heredity and genetics. The patterns of inheritance of plant traits were first described by Gregor Mendel in 1865, and his work has guided scientific plant breeders ever since.

# Chapter 4

# THE MECHANIZED FARM

Most of the farmers throughout the world still practice subsistence farming. They raise just enough plants and tend just enough animals for their own needs. Machines are unable to access uneven terrain such as mountain slopes, and in many areas human and animal labor is far less expensive than machines. Yet mechanized agriculture is used on many of the plains of Latin America, Africa, and Asia.

The style of farming that became traditional to Western cultures in temperate regions was diversified general farming. In this type of farming, various livestock were raised, and fields grew maize (corn), small grains, and soybeans. In the south tobacco, beans, peanuts, maize, small grains, hay and forage crops, and fruit trees were grown. Diversified general farming produced great self-sufficiency for the farmer.

From the 1800s to the late 1900s, technological advances and market forces favored diversified farming. In parts of Europe that trend has largely continued. By the early 2000s in the United States and Canada, however, large-scale agribusiness was forcing many small family farmers out. These North American farms were becoming less diversified as well.

## GREEN REVOLUTION

Starting in the late 1960s, two forces had a tremendous effect on the productivity of global agriculture. First, scientists found ways to grow higher-yielding crops. Second, international programs brought these improved crops and other technologies to farmers in poor countries.

As a result, in what is known as the Green Revolution, staple grains were feeding more people than they ever had. In less-developed countries, wheat yields rose by 200 percent, corn by 150 percent, and rice by over 100 percent. Agriculture developed more rapidly in the Green Revolution than in all previous history. Still other changes occurred in developed countries.

## MORE POWERFUL MACHINES

Mechanization became more common in Western countries shortly after 1850, when a variety of machines came rapidly into use. Patrick Bell in Scotland and Cyrus McCormick in the United States sparked the manufacture of threshing machines. In the 1860s on large farms, steam-powered tractors began to pull plows, cultivators, hay rakes, and grain harvesters. Milking machines appeared as well, beginning the conversion of dairying into an agribusiness.

It was not until the early 1950s, however, that there were more tractors on US farms than workhorses and mules. Tractors now offer many features: cultivators, attachments for forklifts or rotary hoes, pesticide sprayers, GPS, USB ports, and more. Grain augers and large silos, as well as grain dryers, wells, hay baling machines, and "combine" harvesters are also common on mechanized farms. Yet despite advanced mechanization, there are still many high-value crops, including fruits and vegetables, that rely heavily on manual harvesting and other labor.

The great railway networks of Europe and North America were made during the 1800s to gather meat, grain, and other produce from farms and bring it to cities for processing and eating, or to ports for shipping overseas. A surprising amount of this traffic shifted during the 1900s to vehicles for long-haul trucking on the newer network of roads.

## FARM ANIMALS AND DISEASES

Mechanical farm equipment caused a reduction in numbers of draft animals. Still, a large percentage of grain production continues to feed domesticated animals because of the increase in the number of animals raised for meat.

Industrialization of animal production has led to crowds of sheep and cattle being raised without sufficient rangeland. At industrial feedlots, also called confinement operations or “factory farms,” animals are fed with the cheapest available materials. These sprawling sites are claimed to be efficient and cost-saving for the raising of chickens and other domesticated fowl as well. Yet such overcrowded sites may not be sustainable because they generate enormous amounts of feces and other waste, and farmers administer large amounts of antibiotics to animals because close confinement encourages the outbreak of disease.

In modern factory farms, animals are kept close together in small pens and cages, and their manure is hosed out of the barns.

While animals are in confinement, their breeding is also more closely managed. Artificial insemination has become a major factor in their domestication. For example, sperm from about fifty healthy bulls is collected and used to inseminate millions of dairy cows in the United States. Domestic turkeys have to be artificially inseminated. They have been selected for large breast meat to such an extent that by the time they are mature, their big chests make them unable to mate.

Some animals can contract fatal diseases that damage nerve cells and leave a sponge-like pat-

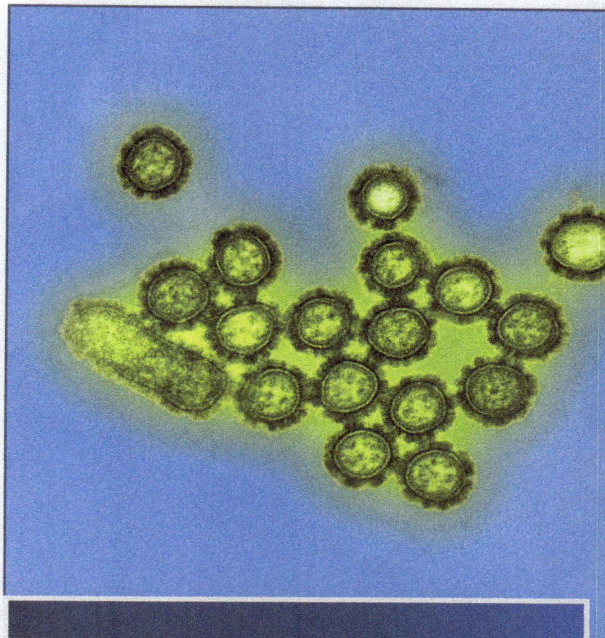

People have been exposed over and over to the diseases of farm animals, and over time some germs like these influenza cells have evolved to infect humans also.

tern of holes in brain tissue. One of the diseases of this group is scrapie, which affects sheep and goats. Another such disease, bovine spongiform encephalopathy (BSE), damages the brain and nerves of cattle. This is why it is commonly known as "mad-cow disease." It spread rapidly in Britain in the late twentieth century because cattle feed was infused with bits of bovine brain, nerve tissue, and other leftovers from slaughterhouses—all intended as an efficient, money-saving "reusing" of protein within the factory-farm system. Government regulations were later enacted to halt that practice, in order to safeguard herds and human lives. Diseases that pass from one kind of animal to another are considered more likely to become infectious to humans. Some researchers have suggested a possible link between

## A JOKE THAT FARMERS TELL

A man comes out from the city in his sports car. He drives somewhat recklessly, causing him to spin out in a ditch. A farmer passing by on a tractor offers to tow the car out. As he's hitching up a towrope, the driver says, "Be careful—that car cost eighty thousand dollars!"

The farmer unhitches the towrope and responds, "Better not risk damaging my tractor. It cost two hundred and fifty thousand dollars."

This joke demonstrates that farming in the current era requires a massive investment. The joke also demonstrates that some people consider farmers to be as poor or unsophisticated today as in earlier times.

BSE and a similar one, Creutzfeldt-Jakob disease, in people.

Humans have caught many diseases from animals. Anthrax, smallpox, tuberculosis, measles, and avian flu are diseases that originated with animals and then mutated to sicken humans.

## BIG CHANGES

A century ago, most farm produce was sold and consumed at nearby homes and the nearest marketing town. Now, farm products may be used thousands of miles away and in a completely changed form. Refrigerated rail cars and steamships were invented decades ago, and now refrigerated trucks keep meat and produce from spoiling on the way to factory or market.

The use of airplanes in spraying crops with chemicals makes protecting the plants more effi-

Large trucks on highways have largely replaced railroads for transporting farm produce from farms to market, often traveling many hundreds of miles.

cient. A plane can spray 1,000 acres (400 hectares) in a matter of minutes. Spraying pesticides and herbicides kills insects and weeds. But spraying is controversial because of harmful effects on wildlife, on other crops, and on human health.

In the 1800s and 1900s, pipes and sprinklers replaced the irrigation techniques of ancient cultures. Irrigation is now the largest single consumer of water on the planet. The interior desert valleys of California, Arizona, and Texas have been converted

Sprinkler systems can be automated to deliver water exactly where it is needed, across entire orchards or feedlots or even a section of land a mile (1.6 km) across.

into oases for crop production. This water can be used intelligently in drip systems and with recycled "gray water" where possible. However, when it is sprayed in high arcs much of it evaporates into the air, and when it is transported in open-air canals water can evaporate and seep into the soil.

In addition, when water used for irrigation comes from underground aquifers, its use is not sustainable. The Ogallala Aquifer, which provides water to the Great Plains states, is being drained of water that will not be able to re-fill until ice from the next Ice Age begins to melt.

Hoses and drip nozzles also work in greenhouses and gardens. True hydroponics (soil-free growing) is practical only for some intensive operations. Yet in the future it may lead the way to sustainable space or lunar colonies.

Chapter 5

# GMO OR NO? MEETING OUR FUTURE NEEDS

We already grow on land or harvest from the sea more than enough food to feed every person on Earth. Unfortunately, natural resources are not managed sustainably or distributed evenly. Trying to distribute food to keep up with an increasing population is agriculture's biggest challenge. Inventions and bumper crops can't bring plenty to all if they're not shared. Yet new technology is too expensive for people in marginalized areas. Distributing crop surpluses to areas suffering from food shortages seems ideal, but transport costs run high. Sometimes cheap imports—even in times of disaster—can bankrupt local farmers.

## MAKING THE MOST

Wasted resources are problems that appropriate technology can address. For one, research scientists are developing biofuels from waste materials of agriculture and forestry. At the same time, however, inefficient products continue to be promoted because of government subsidies. A key example in North America is corn syrup, including high-fructose corn syrup. This product is not as efficiently produced as sugarcane and beet sugar. In addition, numerous health problems (and medical costs) are linked to overuse of these sweeteners.

Thus, corn syrup may be an area where agricultural technology may be doing more harm than good. Yet the US government helps make the price of maize (corn) artificially low, encouraging the use of this syrup in foods. Similar government subsidies keep the price of beef-based products lower than grain-based products, despite the fact that more grain had to be consumed to produce the beef.

Deep tilling is another issue that lets topsoil erode in wind or heavy rains. The new way to plant grain is shallow plowing or no plowing at all, called "no-till" cultivation, to control erosion. Yet a drawback to no-till is the increased use of pesticides and herbicides on many fields.

Efficient use of fertilizers is important, not only to avoid waste but for environmental protection. When excess nitrogen or phosphorus fertilizers leach into rivers and oceans, they trigger massive algae blooms, using up oxygen and causing devastating fish die-offs.

The harvesting of fish with huge purse seines is particularly wasteful, since every fish in the path of these huge nets is caught. In small fishing boats the unwanted fish can be returned to the water. But huge modern fishing boats have motors pulling in purse seines of fish, squid, and sometimes dolphins

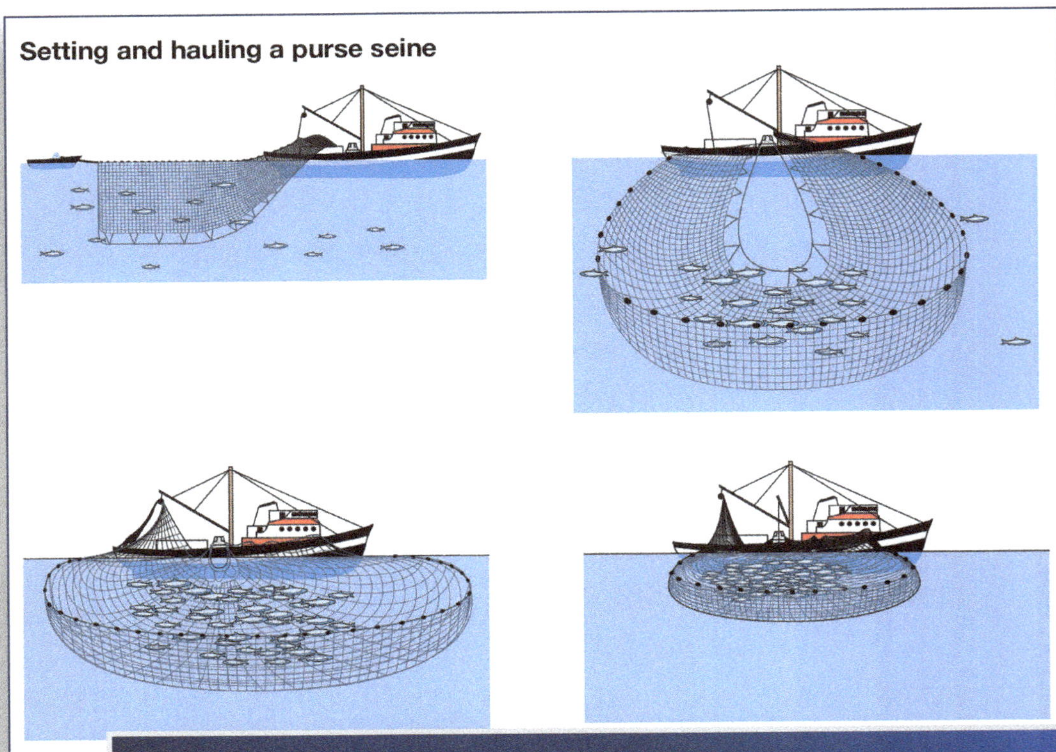


Because giant nets called purse seines catch every animal in their path, bigger is not better when choosing to make a sustainable and selective harvest.

or turtles. Even when the catch is sorted by hand into a ship's freezers, unwanted animals usually do not survive. Waste has increased from 25 percent to 33 percent per catch.

Even more wasteful are dragnets, weighted with heavy steel beams that drag along the sea bottom and chase fish up into the net. Dragnets smash coral and other species that support the marine ecosystem. It's like harvesting apples by driving over apple trees with a bulldozer.

## NEW CROPS: MEETING GOALS

When are new crops better than traditional crops? Often they are part of the answer farmers need for managing work and plans. Some new crops are carefully bred to have more nutrition or to be tough enough to ship to market or to resist disease.

Heritage, or natural, seeds produce offspring like themselves. Modern hybrid varieties of crops are cross-bred between two parents with different qualities, such as a yellow tomato crossed with a disease-resistant red, or a Holstein milk cow bred to an Angus beef bull. Hybrids are often vigorous and strong. But hybrids are not usually kept for many

In this barn, these young Holstein dairy cows not only look alike, but they are all daughters of the same stud bull, bred to their mothers by artificial insemination.

generations because the offspring of a hybrid are not consistent. Instead, the offspring of hybrids can be like any of the grandparents. Once a farmer abandons heritage seeds for hybrids, in other words, additional seeds must be purchased for every future crop.

## ARE GMOS A GOOD OPTION?

Scientists have mapped the genetic blueprint, or genome, of several species. They know the genetic makeup of cattle, chickens, and honeybees, and they can experiment with crossbreeding interspecies genes.

Genetic modification is a new method for creating breeds of plants or animals. In a laboratory, scientists take a piece of DNA from one living thing and insert it into a cell of another species. The idea is to put a gene for one trait, such as a fish's ability to survive cold conditions, into another species, such as a tobacco plant. In this example, the goal may be to create tobacco plants that survive cold weather. The new crop is called a genetically modified organism (GMO).

GMOs are usually marketed as improved breeds. Some seeds are designed so plants will live even if sprayed with herbicide (weed killer). A few GMOs are bred to increase nutrition, such as rice or sweet potatoes with vitamin A.

GMOs don't have genetic diversity like traditional crops, so farmers can lose an entire crop to weather or disease. Terminator seeds are sterile, so new seeds have to be bought to plant every year. Sometimes when the wind blows pollen from a GMO field onto a neighboring field, crops there experience sterility, lower yield, and lower nutrition.

Monsanto, an American company that produces GMO seeds, has sued such neighboring farmers regularly for planting its GMO canola without paying for seed, even when pollen was wind-blown from another farmer's GMO field.

GMO animals have caused problems as well. GMO Atlantic salmon escape from crowded, mis-managed fish farms and spread diseases into wild salmon stocks. Most important, there have not been studies of the effects of eating GMO food over long periods of time. Research has not addressed all the consumer fears of so-called "Franken-foods" and "Franken-fish." As a result, most European governments have resisted GMO sales, as have some US consumer groups.

## E-AGRICULTURE

E-agriculture is the combination of electronic information (e.g., in computers) with agricultural production. It helps with growing and harvesting food, as well as marketing and distributing it. E-agriculture includes sensors, computers, Internet-linked networks, mobile phones and applications (apps), and also radios, satellites, and closed-circuit televisions.

## ROUNDUP-READY CANOLA

Canola was selectively bred in Canada from rapeseed, a field grain related to kale. Seeds from both canola and rapeseed are crushed for oil to use in cooking. Monsanto, an agricultural and chemical corporation, patented a genetically engineered (GMO) version of canola that survives being sprayed with Roundup, a weed killer Monsanto developed that contains glyphosate. Monsanto has marketed Roundup Ready canola since 1997, despite controversy surrounding its nutrition, productivity, and safety.

These protesters gathered in Malmo, Sweden, in 2016 to protest against GMOs and unethical practices by international corporations marketing seeds.

They assist with innovative approaches to farming, like greenhouse sensors and Bluetooth controllers for vents or drip irrigation.

They also help farmers pay their taxes, plan next year's crops, and safeguard against the theft of equipment and fuel. More than a million commercial firms are engaged in agricultural marketing and processing.

## HUNGER AROUND THE WORLD

There are more than 820 million chronically hungry people in the world. Most live in sub-Saharan Africa, southern Asia, and Latin America. Yet even in developed countries, many people do not have reliable access to food. In 2015, nearly 13 percent of Americans were designated as "food insecure." Much of the world's food is not produced and distributed evenly.

Governments have attempted to support more stable food supplies when facing drought, flood, and other natural disasters. They use technologies to support better planning and investments in sustainability, food storage, and the transportation and sale of healthy foods.

On World Food Day, October 16, 2017, Pope Francis attended a meeting of the Food and Agriculture Organization (FAO) of the United Nations.

The World Food Summit attempted to address malnutrition in 1996. That work was continued in 2000, when one of the United Nations' Millennium Development Goals was to reduce by half the number of people suffering from hunger by 2015. That goal was not met, although many countries reduced hunger and malnourishment.

Advocates for sustainability and environmental protection view agricultural technologies from different viewpoints. Some want our existing agriculture to be more efficient, including the production of sugar, corn syrup, and meat. Meanwhile, we also rely on the invention of new medicines to combat rising levels of diabetes, heart disease, and obesity. Yet evidence suggests that meat-heavy diets are one of our gravest environmental concerns. Even efficient farms require enormous quantities of grain to raise cattle, pigs, and poultry. That same amount of grain, in contrast, could feed large numbers of people directly.

In addition, we should factor in the diesel fuel and gasoline upon which our present system depends, as well as clean water, as far more of these resources are needed for meat than grain production. A more sustainable path forward might be support for vegan or at least vegetarian diets, by reducing meat consumption in favor of plant products. Yet our appetite for meat appears to be increasing, not only in North America but also among the increasingly affluent classes of China. In the future, will we need to see poor people starve in order to satiate wealthier people's desire for meat?

By 2030, an additional two billion people will need to be fed with land and water resources that are made more fragile and unpredictable by pollution, unsustainable use of fuel and other resources, and the scientifically proven threats of global warming. Major innovations in agricultural technologies, ranging from tools and industrial equipment to sustainable civil engineering and transportation networks, will be needed to meet these challenges.

# GLOSSARY

**AGRICULTURE** Growing plants and raising animals for food, cloth, and other products.

**AGRONOMY** A branch of agriculture dealing with field-crop production and soil management.

**AQUIFER** A layer of rock or sand that can absorb and hold water below the surface.

**ARABLE LAND** An area of Earth's surface that is fit for or used for the growing of crops.

**ARTIFICIAL INSEMINATION** Taking sperm from a male and inserting it into a female to make her pregnant, without mating.

**CONFINEMENT OPERATION** A site using a "factory farm" system in which animals are kept in overcrowded conditions, with the goals of maximizing efficiency and profit.

**CROP ROTATION** The system of planting a series of different crops on the same soil in a sequence of seasons, to control weeds and pests and to avoid depleting the soil.

**FALLOW SYSTEM** Allowing some land to rest, without planting crops on it, during the growing season; sometimes fallow land is part of a system of crop rotation.

**FOOD PROCESSING** The transformation of ingredients, by physical or chemical changes, into food; or the transformation of food into marketable food products such as packaged snacks or bottled drinks.

**FOOD INSECURE** Being unable to access or afford enough food on a regular, consistent basis.

**GENE** Part of a plant or animal's DNA that determines a trait such as hair color or potential size.

**GENETICALLY MODIFIED ORGANISM (GMO)** A living thing created by surgically inserting a gene from a plant or animal into the DNA of another plant or animal.

**HERBICIDE** A chemical used to kill unwanted plants.

**INDUSTRIAL FEEDLOT** A site, also called a "factory farm," where large populations of animals, such as cattle or pigs, are confined and fed in order to fatten them for slaughter as quickly as possible.

**MULCH** Materials such as straw, leaves, or seaweed used to cover the ground around plants in a garden or orchard.

**ORGANIC FARMING** Agriculture undertaken without the use of chemical fertilizers, pesticides, and herbicides.

**PESTICIDE** A chemical used to kill unwanted insects.

**PLANTATION** A large area of land that employs resident labor to cultivate a commercial crop, such as palm oil, coffee, or bananas.

**POLDER** A tract of lowland reclaimed from a body of water, often the sea, through drainage and the construction of dikes.

**PREY** An animal that typically gets hunted by a predator (an animal, such as a shark or a human, that hunts other animals).

**PURSE SEINE** A massive fishing net that is dragged from a boat to capture large numbers of fish.

**RATION** A serving of food organized by a planner and issued to a worker or soldier, usually a day's food.

**SELECTIVE BREEDING** The human-controlled breeding of animals or plants in order to produce offspring that possess desirable qualities, such as a particular size, color, or flavor.

**SLAUGHTERHOUSE** A structure where animals are killed and butchered and where the meat and meat byproducts are packaged and inspected.

**STERILE/STERILITY** In animals, an inability to produce offspring. In food preparation and cleaning, these words indicate clean conditions where germs cannot spread or reproduce.

**SUSTAINABILITY** A state in which human actions are helping to preserve, balance, and sustain an entire community—not only human life but also plants and animals in the natural world.

***TERRA PRETA DO INDIO*** Fertile, human-altered soil of a dark color in the Brazilian rainforest.

**VEGAN** A person who does not eat any animal products, including meat, fish, dairy, and eggs; a vegan diet is completely plant based.

**VEGETARIAN** A person who does not eat meat and fish but may eat some other animal products, such as dairy or eggs.

**WEIR** A fence or enclosure set in a waterway for capturing fish.

# FOR FURTHER READING

Berry, Wendell. *The Unsettling of America: Culture & Agriculture.* Berkeley, CA: Counterpoint Press, 2015.

Blythman, Joanna. *Swallow This: Serving Up the Food Industry's Darkest Secrets.* London, UK: Fourth Estate, 2015.

Davis, Garth. *Proteinaholic: How Our Obsession with Meat Is Killing Us and What We Can Do About It.* New York, NY: HarperOne, 2015.

Druker, Steven M. *Altered Genes, Twisted Truth: How the Venture to Genetically Engineer Our Food Has Subverted Science, Corrupted Government, and Systematically Deceived the Public.* Fairfield, IA: Clear River Press, 2015.

Francis, Richard C. *Domesticated: Evolution in a Man-Made World.* New York, NY: W.W. Norton, 2015.

Lynas, Mark. *Seeds of Science: Why We Got It So Wrong on GMOs.* London, UK: Bloomsbury, 2018.

McQuaid, John. *Tasty: The Art and Science of What We Eat.* Toronto, ON: Simon & Schuster, 2015.

Nestle, Marion. *Food Politics: How the Food Industry Influences Nutrition and Health.* Oakland, CA: University of California Press, 2013.

Ogle, Maureen. *In Meat We Trust: An Unexpected History of Carnivore America.* Boston, MA: Houghton Mifflin Harcourt, 2013.

Schlosser, Eric. *Fast Food Nation: The Dark Side of the All-American Meal.* Boston, MA: Mariner Books, 2012.

Shiva, Vandana. *Staying Alive: Women, Ecology, and Development.* Berkeley, CA: North Atlantic Books, 2016.

Shiva, Vandana. *Who Really Feeds the World?: The Failures of Agribusiness and the Promise of Agroecology.* Berkeley, CA: North Atlantic Books, 2016.

## WEBSITES

**Food and Agriculture Organization of the United Nations (FAO)**
http://www.fao.org/home/en/
Twitter: @FAOnews; Instagram: @unfao

**Science Buddies**
https://www.sciencebuddies.org/science-fair-projects/project-ideas/agricultural-technology
Twitter, Facebook: @ScienceBuddies

**US Department of Agriculture**
https://www.usda.gov
Twitter, Facebook: @USDA; Instagram: @usdagov

# INDEX